The Manager's Mentor

THE MANAGER'S MENTOR

Les McIlroy

Centennial College Press
Toronto, Ontario
2020

Published by
Centennial College Press
951 Carlaw Avenue
Toronto, ON M4K 3M2
https://centennialcollegepress.com/

The original edition included the following CIP data:
Canadian Cataloguing in Publication Data
McIlroy, Les, 1934-
The manager's mentor : simple answers to complicated questions
ISBN 1-55228-016-0
1. Management. I. Title   HD31.M234   1998   658   C97-932801-2

Originally published by turnerbooks. This Centennial College Press edition
published by arrangement with Jennifer McIlroy.

*To Ruth for her support and counsel,
and Jennifer for her help*

CONTENTS

INTRODUCTION

I miss my father. He shot them if he loved them. He didn't speak in elevators. He avoided fads. He knew a hoax when he saw one.

And he knew how to mentor the best out of everyone.

He wrote *The Manager's Mentor* after years of following his instincts in business and people management. He'd been excavating the inner opera in people as an avid member of Hi-Y in Ottawa, a volunteer basketball coach for the YMCA, an early entrepreneur, a nimble offensive player for the Carleton University Ravens football team, one of the best canoe, swimming, bonfire sing-along camp counsellors in southern Ontario, and as *the* best bedtime story teller, ever. He lived it, believed it, and then wrote it.

I don't point out his business experience as the source of his acumen. Most certainly, that acumen was honed in the many circumstances he encountered as a writer, trainer, advertising professional, political strategist, manager, VP, Chief of Staff, and President. I rather point out his mind and his talent, innate and unique to him: his genuine kindness paired with incisive knowledge.

His lessons are timeless.

It's the timelessness that explains why his words endure, as relevant now as they were more than two decades ago.

That is why I miss my father and why the world misses Les. He'd have loved to see how his words continue to inspire emerging managers, some still in elementary school when *The Manager's Mentor* was first published, and others who've been on the job awhile but need a smart, compassionate mentor in their corner.

JENNIFER A. MCILROY
2020

FOREWORD

There is much to say on the subject of management, and many authors would be tempted to write a very long book. But long books don't get read by busy managers. They just sit on the shelf and look impressive. My aim, however, is to share thoughts and ideas with you, not simply decorate your office.

Putting all these on paper made me realize that, had I been motivated to do so, I would have written almost the same book three or four decades ago. Managing, you see, doesn't change very much over the years. Yes, the titles change. The communications vehicles change. But people don't. Their fears, egos, ambitions, needs and hopes stay the same. Each of us comes into an organization with no memory or experience. We all bring to work every day the same human strengths and frailties our parents and grandparents did.

We used to delegate; now we empower. In either case, if we do it well, the results are the same. Employee performance rises to meet the manager's expectations.

Perhaps social media will replace the old workplace grapevine, but the result won't be any more or less accurate. I doubt it will be much faster.

Which means that, as a manager, you never have to wait for a new development or a new technological era for your excitement. The excitement is in the people and leading their differences onto a common path for some part of most days.

There is an old Sumerian saying: "Because you understand one, you think you understand two, because one and one make two." But in management you must also understand "and."

You will not find spiritual uplift in this book. Nor will you discover pithy aphorisms for the bulletin board. You will, however, find some common-sense approaches to the job of managing organizations through people.

Do not be afraid of simple solutions to problems. The highest compliment that can be paid to an idea is: "That's so obvious. Why didn't I think of that?"

The Manager's Mentor

IN THE
BEGINNING

It all begins with marketing. Not just business, but much of life. And the Golden Rule is: Treat the customer well.

In all our relationships every day, we have customers. Some we want to buy our products. Some we want to buy our ideas. Some we want to listen to our advice on why they should be home by ten on school nights.

In each case the customer has needs and interests, ones that might not be the same as ours. Our job is to find a way to explain our product, idea, rule or plea so that it fills a need of the customer—not always easy but always the one sure route to success.

The "customer satisfaction" proponents embrace this thinking in their work. The idea of "internal customers" allows customer satisfaction to move off the front lines and into the offices, warehouses and accounting departments. Everybody has a customer who must be satisfied, the argument goes, whether the customer is the person at the next desk waiting for the day's time sheets or the purchasing vice-president for a Big Three auto firm.

If we think of everybody we meet as a customer, it soon becomes a habit. What's the risk? Well, you might be more pleasant or considerate of somebody than you really have to be to get by. Hardly a shame.

This book is about how you can use this marketing concept in a host of situations. It won't always be obvious, but the marketing approach will never be more than one layer down anywhere in this volume.

When you remember that the son of the receptionist at the medical clinic is graduating this year and you mention it to her, that's marketing. She feels good, you feel good. It's an improvement over the usual impersonal atmosphere.

In the old days, when most companies had receptionists who sat at desks in the front lobby, marketing was an art practised by good salespeople. A smart one had the name, birthday, names of children and other data recorded in the call book. He or she would check the listing, walk through the door and say, "Good morning, Mary. That new grandson of yours must be about ready to walk, isn't he?"

Sure, maybe recording personal data was a bit cold-blooded, but so what? The effort didn't hurt anyone, but it sure helped when there was a traffic jam of salespeople waiting for an audience with somebody on the other side of the wall behind the receptionist. So if marketing is all that important, you ask, doesn't it make sense to start this book with the *Marketing Plan?*

No two words in the language have ever been granted more importance, more mystery, more cachet than Marketing Plan. Only the favoured few from selected business schools are supposed to know about the Marketing Plan.

Now, before we deal with the *Great Marketing Plan Hoax*, let me share some thoughts on other subjects.

VISION AND MISSION

In recent years many organizations have rushed to develop Mission statements and Vision statements. We often see the results hanging on the wall in branch offices, the frame dusty and the glass greasy and streaked. Unfortunately this is often the state of both Mission and Vision within the organization—neglected.

In most cases organizations have made the mistake of thinking of Mission and Vision as one-time exercises. The management team goes to a resort for the weekend and works them out. Then Public Relations and Human Resources "communicate" them to employees and feature the new words in the annual report. The end.

To be done right, Mission and Vision development must involve at various times employees, customers, community stakeholders, suppliers and others.

Developing and benefiting from Mission and Vision work is a process, not a continuing act. It is also work that must have the total commitment of the senior executives of the organization. *Every day.*

Why bother?

Effective Mission and Vision statements are articulate expressions of what makes people proud to work for your organization. They challenge employees, promise customers, entice new workers.

If a fire department "puts out fires," it may well be an excellent force. If its Mission is to "save lives and protect our neighbours' property," the firefighters probably walk taller.

Similarly a Vision for the future in an organization can create a goal, an aspiration shared by all. Does it matter?

Albert Einstein said, "I believe in intuition and inspiration … at times I feel I am right while not knowing the reason … imagination is more important than knowledge. For knowledge is limited, whereas imagination embraces the entire world, stimulating progress, giving birth to evolution."

This is why effective organizations develop Vision statements. The challenge to the entire workforce is to close the gap between their imagined best and today's performance. It's a task that can be undertaken. It's a task that can be measured and rewarded. It's the model against which all plans can be tested.

A good Vision statement allows us to create the future, not simply wait for it to arrive.

The Mission statement is our daily guideline on the way to that future.

Most organizations need assistance in the creation of Mission and Vision statements to make them dynamic, day-to-day tools in the workplace and marketplace. Look to an organization you admire and find out who helped it.

TIME IS A PIECE
OF SOMEONE'S LIFE

There is rarely an acceptable excuse for being late. Think of time as a piece of the other person's life. It is their most precious commodity. There'd better be a very good reason if one treats that life lightly.

We all know people who are always late. If they keep you waiting once or twice, let them know gently how you feel about it. The next time they are late, be gone, absent, not to be found. They'll get the message.

If your boss is always late, you may have to put up with it. However, do not gather the rest of your gang in the office to await the boss's always-late arrival. Tell them to be on the alert to drop tools when the boss arrives, but to keep on working in the meantime. If you can't teach the boss good manners, it doesn't mean you have to let production suffer.

If you are going to be late, phone. Now that everyone carries a mobile phone, there's no reason you can't advise the people waiting that you are tied up in a traffic jam caused by a multi-car collision on the only artery into town. Lesser reasons are unacceptable and send a clear signal that either (a) you have little respect for the waiting people and their lives; or (b) you are so insecure that you need to walk in last to enjoy some attention.

Think about it the next time someone is late. Then think about that person thinking about you if *you* are late.

RUNNING
USEFUL MEETINGS

This book will touch on meetings a number of times. Meetings are so much a part of business we must examine them from several viewpoints. Let's look at some of the ways to run meetings effectively.

First, always start on time. If the meeting isn't important enough to start promptly, don't hold it.

Don't stop the meeting to bring latecomers up to date. They are the sinners, not the folks who respected the invitation. If latecomers feel left out, tough.

Define the purpose of the meeting in the first sixty seconds. Do that by answering aloud this question: Why are these people in this place at this time? (You should have answered this question to yourself before deciding to call the meeting and whom to invite.)

Don't let people sit in the same place at every meeting. Thwart this by changing where *you* sit. Control does not come with position at the table.

Don't let participants take notes for at least the first ten minutes of the meeting. You want undivided attention to the problem. You don't want a record of who said what. You want thinking, concentration on the subject at hand and courtesy to all participants. If participants need to carry away a written record, you can stop later and let the group do a summary.

Suppose you call a meeting of department managers. You must make it clear, if a manager chooses to send a substitute, that person must bring the manager's authority and power of attorney with him or her. You are not holding a meeting as a briefing for an absent manager who then gets to have the meeting convened again. Favourite trick of the insecure. Very prevalent in government.

More about meetings later.

THE COMMUNICATIONS POWER GRID

For planning, teaching, involving and inspiring, no single communications tool comes close to the Power Grid. This simple tool allows the expert to improve precision, and the novice to learn and see the big picture. And it's fun to use.

Here's how it works. Given a communications-planning task, write the audiences for the message you wish to deliver along the top of the grid. Down the side, write in the media that could be used to reach those audiences.

Don't worry about being perfect. The grid will prod you to get better. The colleagues you enlist to help with the grid will also help you. Just try to get the basic audiences down and at least the most obvious possible media. Include meetings and one-to-one presentations.

Now go down each line of the grid. At each media heading ask, "Is there some way we could use this medium to reach this audience?" For example, let's suppose the first audience on your grid is the general public and your first media line is television. You ask, "Is there some way we can use television to reach the general public?" You might say yes to this.

As for one-to-one meetings you will likely conclude they are not useful for reaching the general public.

Do your best to ask and answer the question each square in the grid "asks." Be inventive. Have fun.

Invite your communications team or the executive committee or a group of middle managers and new employees to get involved in the grid. Then watch its potency begin to show.

Ideally you blow the grid up on a large screen. First, ask the group if there are any audiences or media they think should be added. Don't argue with the suggestions, just add them. The impractical ideas will correct themselves out of existence later on. Let people get involved.

The assembled group has now become a communications-planning team.

Walk through the grid one square at a time. Ask people to think about how to use each medium for each audience. Few will be able to resist being involved. Remember the old complaint "Everybody thinks they are communications experts"? That's exactly what you want. If only one new idea comes from a group, the plan has been enriched.

More than that, every time a group works with the grid the players become more accomplished. That means your colleagues are learning more about communications. They become part of the plan; the plan is now the child of everybody.

Here are a couple of examples of the synergy the grid generates:

(1) In a top-level presentation of communications for a new government-employee-benefit program, the department minister was intrigued with the grid. After a few minutes' study he said, "There's no checkmark beside 'direct mail.' Why don't we use pay-envelope inserts? That's like mail." And they did.

(2) A major corporation won a prestigious award for "total quality" work. The management wanted to communicate this accomplishment. They used the grid in planning. One of the questions it asked was, "Is there some way we can use advertising to tell about this award?" The apparent answer would be no. The corporation's advertising strategy was product-oriented and this was basically a corporate story.

Then somebody from Advertising who was invited to the meeting said, "What if the product advertising mentioned the award as a reason to believe our product claims?"

Why not? The next pool of commercials was strengthened with mention of the award.

That happened because the total quality leaders used the grid to involve the entire management team.

The grid on page 16 is the one used to talk about the total quality award. It's about as simple as these things get. Nevertheless, some smart things happened along the way with this grid.

Forcing the question about reaching the general public with advertising led to a copy modification. Similarly, when people ran across and up and down the grid, they asked, "Why not direct mail to pensioners on this one?" Somebody else said, "While we are at it, let's ask them about ideas they have for improvement." Another voice offered, "Why not a suggestion system for pensioners? They're out and about more than we are and might see useful things." And so on. (The pensioner-suggestion system doesn't show on the grid, but it will in the company.)

The idea of using media releases tailored to specific regions came from the grid. First, the importance of the public in the hometowns of regional offices was identified. Then the audience "regional public" was placed on the grid, and that generated the ideas of regionalized releases.

The trick to using the grid is always be inclusive in

listing audiences and media. Any that are not practical will eliminate themselves during discussion on the grid.

If you like, as I have done on occasion, you can bring the grid back for a second discussion with rough costs written right on it. There is no simpler way to let people see what they are paying to reach one audience compared with another.

The grid is a way to bring "outside the box" thinking right into the boxes on the screen in your meeting room. It invites the inclusion of the latest media possibilities.

Finally the Power Grid is an exceptional, evocative instrument if you make it so. You have to bring "Why not?" to the table rather than "It won't work." You can be confident the Power Grid will adjust itself to the level of sophistication of the organization. I have used it successfully in plans for large international advertising agencies, major government departments, leading public relations firms, YMCAs, political campaigns, trade associations and a six-person unit trying to get attention within a large corporation.

Fortunately the grid tends to choose its own wielders. People who are afraid of the challenge of new ideas don't use the grid twice.

I hope you use it as often and as fruitfully as I have.

MEDIUM	Customers	Employees	Prospects	Shareholders	General Public	Union Leadership	Pensioners	Regional Public
General News Release				X				
Paid Advertising	X		X	X				
Meeting		X			X			
Fax		X						
One-to-One	X				X			
Direct Mail	X		X	X		X		
Employee Bulletin		X				X		
Trade Press-Release	X		X					
Regional Press-Release							X	
Internet								

The Communications Power Grid

JUDGING ADVERTISING

Assuming advertising material has been prepared to meet a specific strategy or tactic, here are some things to remember about the judging and approval process:

(1) If you use an advertising agency and the people in your company really and truly reach an impasse over whether the new creative is right, go with the agency. You owe them that respect or you should find another agency. This is very important.

(2) Always read television commercial storyboards by the pictures only. Cover the words. If you need the words to understand the commercial, then you are looking at a radio commercial. Don't send a radio commercial with pictures to do a job on television.

(3) Pay a lot of attention to first-class large-base research. Don't pay much attention to focus groups, and don't pay any attention at all to focus groups unless you are actually present for the group session.

Focus groups started out as a way to fine-tune questions for proper research. How they became an end in themselves is a mystery. Maybe, as a guide to executions of advertising, focus groups have a place. "Can you read this headline? Is it big enough?" are questions where a focus group might be helpful. We must always remember that the opinion of one or two people on any subject does not become more valid because it is stated behind a one-way mirror. So stop making a science out of interpretations based on 0.00000001 percent of the consumer public.

(4) Make sure your agency is making money on your account. The temptation is always great to ask for a little more marketing support from your advertising agency, then a little more. That costs money (resources). You want the agency making advertising, not trying to find ways to cut corners to meet your escalating demands.

Your agency is one of your partners. Don't you want your partners to do well?

(5) Be generous with advertising-research money for the agency. The better the agency, the more they will want to use research as part of the creative process. Give the agency support in this effort. And make sure your

original agreement with the agency includes a note on who pays for advertising research.

APPROVING ADVERTISING MATERIALS

Now and then new advertising is presented by your advertising agency. It may be advertising for products or for the corporate image or crisisresponse work.

If more than one person represents the client, here is a rule to follow: the clients' reps must comment in reverse order of rank. The most junior person speaks first and so on. That makes it impossible to follow the boss's line. It also allows senior executives to appraise the talent of the juniors. Don't make this a casual happening. Make it a rule.

Another rule: whether there is one or a dozen client-side reviewers looking at advertising (doesn't matter if it is print, direct marketing, radio or television, the same rule applies), state in the first two sentences whether you are in favour of rejecting the advertising or accepting it, perhaps with some positive criticism. The agency, or the writer or designer, needs to know right now if they have a success. Don't wander all over the place and end up with a half hearted okay for the creative material.

If it is not on strategy, if it doesn't reach out to potential customers and grab them by the arm, start over. A bad idea fixed with patches, however clever, never succeeds.

If you are a marketer, you owe it to the creative people to jump for joy when they hit the target. If it turns out the advertising doesn't work as well as you hoped, you must share the disappointment with the creators. Only when you say "yes" at the outset do you get to say "we did it" when stuff works.

You will get better advertising if the writers trust that you have the nerve to love their work out loud.

RESEARCH

You must always, before committing to research, ask yourself, "What am I going to do with the results?" This will encourage you to do applied research. The other kind, which is common, is the stuff that is interesting to know but that you do not have resources to exploit.

For instance, you may find it informative to learn the exact media-viewing habits of the population organized by sex, age and so on.

Informative, yes, but if your advertising budget is less than two million dollars, you can't do much about buying the segmentation media you would need in a perfect world. Better to have spent the research money making sure your existing advertising is delivering the message exactly as you intended.

So first think about it, then do all the research you can afford. If you can't afford good research, don't do any. Marketers are led astray every day by "invalid" research—research badly designed or with too small a statistical base to support the conclusions. The problem is that once an undertaking is labelled "research" it assumes an aura of credibility it may not have earned. That leads to lousy decisions.

As I previously suggested, the best example of this is the whole field of focus groups. These devices came into being to help design real research projects, to check people's understanding of some jargon, to test the clarity of questions. Sometimes they were even merely pilots for the real thing—the field research.

Somewhere along the line a budget squeeze urged some marketers to use focus-group results as if they were actual research. This may be the greatest single sin committed by marketing specialists in the twentieth century.

Today otherwise responsible executives throw focus-group results into presentations and sales meetings like hand grenades. Bah. Humbug.

Focus groups can help on some projects, but in the main they are only useful when you want a quick counter to a boss who says, "My wife/husband tells me the people she/he knows all like Italian food (or radio advertising, or trust companies)." Hit the boss with a focus group.

Oh, and there's one other excellent use. As part of your customer-satisfaction work, get some real live customers into a focus group and stick company executives on the other side of the one-way glass. The experience helps the executives believe that not every customer is satisfied (many dissatisfied customers don't tell you if you don't ask).

Here are some easy rules for dealing with research:

(1) Find a professional tesearch organization to advise and conduct your research.

(2) Tell the researcher what you want to know. Let the researcher tell you how to find it out. Hiring a research organization is like engaging an electrician to wire your house—you tell him where you want illumination and let him take care of the wiring.

(3) Insist on doing *quality* research rather than *lots* of research.

(4) Look for partners to share the cost. Two noncompetitive marketers might together be able to afford a national survey, instead of just the region or two you alone could afford.

(5) Before starting your research, check to see what's on the various information bases available to you. There is likely information sitting out there free of charge allowing you to either avoid spending time and money on your own research or to really sharpen its focus.

CONSUMER RESEARCH

You don't have to know much about research as a manager.

You do have to know people who know lots and lots about research.

You also have to know when to call on those people.

Research is the way we read the consumer's mind. It is the cheapest insurance against disaster we can buy; it should be considered an ingredient of every product.

Think of it this way: in a perfect world we could sit down with each potential consumer, tell her/him about our product, answer questions and make the sale. In the real world, research is a substitute for those conversations (so is advertising, about which I address more elsewhere).

You can research attitudes, advertising, colours, packaging, smells, promotion ideas, premiums, signage, governments, trade sectors, in-store traffic and other aspects of your business. At various times you will want to do research in many of these areas.

Start the research with yourself. Ask this question: "Is there information I need to improve my business effectiveness?" Next, ask: "Are there research methods that could help me?" Then make a priority list and do what you can afford, in order.

Now, one of the reasons we need to know smart research professionals is to help answer the second of the two questions above. You and I may assume certain information cannot be elicited through research. We may be wrong. The experts will help. Or we may feel a particular research project is unaffordable. The experts may be able to suggest ways to do it at a reasonable price: perhaps another, noncompetitive company will be happy to share the costs of a survey that's unaffordable for each of you separately.

So get in bed with a top-flight research company. Don't let any buying policy or financial rules force you to jump around from supplier to supplier. Your researcher is like your advertising agency—you want these people as colleagues. Ideas we sometimes don't know enough to ask for can be sales-curve changers.

(When I worked for a company that thought every

research project should go to tender, threatening the continuity of thought we needed, I had the advertising agency subcontract the research to the company we wanted.)

With this general attitude in mind, here are some further thoughts about research, in no particular order:

(1) Read the research chapter in David Ogilvy's book, *Ogilvy on Advertising*. (Then, if you haven't already, read the rest of the book. This tip alone will repay you for buying my book.)

(2) Use focus groups with care. Always use a trained moderator who understands the purpose of the research. Always be present or have the top marketing person attend. Agree in advance about how you will interact with the moderator during the session; you may, for instance, want to pursue an idea that arises unexpectedly. (It only costs extra coffee to bring the backroom gang from Finance and Production to some focus groups. They might learn more about consumers and the incredible varieties in which they appear. And they will feel part of things.)

(3) Look for co-op opportunities to make research affordable. When I was with the Canadian government, we did a study in the U.S. to help determine what factors affected decisions to travel to Canada. The study cost more than one million dollars but created a benchmark for later research by provinces and municipalities, as well as providing its initial yield of insights. No single tourism business in Canada could have afforded such a large

study. The provinces paid a share of the cost to get information specific to their region.

Similarly, the omnibus studies offered by major research groups make broad-scale research affordable by sharing the costs of telephones, staff and administration with a number of clients, each of which gets private results for specific questions asked.

You can do these kinds of co-op projects by finding your own partners. Even within your own industry you may be better off with all the companies knowing more about the consumer than you do now. This is particularly true if your industry needs to talk to government.

(4) As in research in general, look for existing information before spending your own money. It is amazing how much useful data is already in the public domain. Find it. Use it either in place of original research or to focus your research.

(5) Again, always insist that any proposal for research starts by answering this question: "What will we do with the results?" This guarantees your staff (or agencies) don't get into theoretical research. Only applied research need apply.

SHOOT THEM
IF YOU LOVE THEM

People love to have their pictures taken. They thrill to the idea of being recorded for posterity. Taking pictures and giving them to people is the cheapest, most effective promotion activity there is.

When customers visit your plant, take photos. Send them digital copies or, if you want to make them feel really special, old-fashioned physical prints. Let customers see themselves examining your quality-control lab.

Always take pictures at receptions or dinners for customers. Get a first-rate photographer. Tell the shooter in advance which customers you must have pictures of. Let the photographer do the pushing and interrupting—nobody ever really minds.

Those who tell you they don't care about pictures are not telling the truth. Check out the walls in their private offices, or their rec rooms, should you visit their homes. You'll see handshakes and speechmaking and award acceptances all recorded.

If you are doing political or charity work, always make sure your contributors are photographed with any celebrity in sight. I once got ten company presidents who'd previously been unreachable to come have a drink and be photographed with film star Arlene Dahl.

Depending on the importance of the relationship and your own budget, you can send physical prints framed or unframed, sterling silver or plastic.

So just know this: any sales promotion event that does not include a professional photographer is a huge opportunity missed.

BREAK DOWN
THE WALLS

Convention often prevents us from communicating easily and effectively. Habits and past experience have built real and psychological walls between us and our audience. Here are some ways to smash through the walls and be a human being.

Never sit behind your desk to carry on a conversation with somebody who has come to see you. Have a seat *beside* your desk for visitors. Or sit on the desk on the other person's side. Maybe go down the hall for coffee. If you have the space, make a section of your office into a discussion area. Whatever. Just don't hide behind that desk "wall" and make the other human being have to scale it to get to you, and vice versa.

Lots of smart executives have their desks facing *away* from the door so when you or I walk in and they turn around, the desk does not come between.

Because if you have to hide, you ain't ready.

When making stand-up presentations, go out into the audience as far as you can. In a boardroom, walk along the side of the room and look at your slides with the audience from time to time. The less we seem like a lecturer the more we communicate and sell.

Use wireless microphones whenever you can on a platform. They let you walk around without tethers. I re-member a speaker who sat in an easy chair at the front edge of the stage because he had injured his back. He was almost a member of the audience and effective because of it.

At times the setup of a meeting makes it difficult to break down the walls—for example, you might be stuck behind a fixed mike on a panel. Don't criticize the ar-rangements—if you didn't get them changed in advance, don't waste the audience's time with your problems. Do say that, at the end of the panel meeting, you are going to step over to such and such a corner to talk to anybody who wants more exchange. That way you break down the wall at the earliest opportunity.

So watch for walls. Smash through them.

HOW TO RUN
A PROBLEM-SOLVING
MEETING

From time to time you have to bring people together to sort out a specific problem that has sprung up. It might be a communications breakdown between Marketing and Manufacturing; it might be a battle between Sales and Finance over quarterly forecasts. Whatever the problem, you want it behind you so the organization can get on with business.

The meeting you call to solve a specific problem is different from most others. The way you manage the meeting is also different.

Understand—we are not talking here about brainstorming or regular meetings of managers or teams; they have their own rules.

Here we are dealing with the meeting designed to bring people together to find a solution to a problem.

Here are the rules:

(1) Only those involved with the problem should be participants in the meeting. Those who are not stakeholders react differently from those who are, and so cannot be change agents in these circumstances. This may mean that a problem identified in, say, the regular monthly planning meeting, may be dealt with in a separate, subsidiary meeting.

(2) Start the meeting with a plain statement of why the meeting is happening and why now. "We are meeting today, before the financial forecast is due, to talk about the problem we've had preparing it. We need to find some solution."

(3) Then ask a question directed to the group as a whole, not any individual, that begins with "Who?", "What?" or "When?"—for example, "Who can explain the problem to us?"

(4) Let the question hang in the air. Do not elaborate. Do not repeat. Do not look to any one person to answer.

(5) Within thirty seconds someone will answer. The group will not tolerate silence. Your job is to know that and wait.

(6) Once the first answer comes back, guide the discussion in a normal fashion. You are in control because

you have made a neutral start. Now you can lead without being involved. Let the participants solve the problem.

(7) Keep asking questions, and now direct them to individuals to make sure everyone participates. "What do think of that, Mary?" "Would that help you, Bob?"

(8) If appropriate, use a flip chart, but let the participants wield the marker. You want to concentrate on leading, not writing.

(9) Use "Why?" a lot to force people to think about the source of the problem. But don't be afraid to take a backseat and let the meeting flow without you. You will learn a lot and be able to slide in with the right question from time to time.

(10) Look for small agreements along the way. "Would we all agree with that definition of the problem?"

(11) When ideas for solutions begin to suggest themselves—and they will—look for buy-in. "Would that work?" "Do we want to try it?" "Will everybody give it their best shot?"

(12) Summarize the agreements for the group.

Like most management work, steering problem-solving meetings becomes easier with practice. Use these rules as a beginning guide.

MEDIA INTERVIEWS

Most senior managers will be interviewed by the media at some time. It may be because of a new plant opening or a plant closing. Perhaps the media want to hear about a new product or discuss the product recall you have just announced. It may be a welcome or unwelcome opportunity.

Certainly you will be more cautious in interviews about disasters than in those hailing a record year. But whatever the situation, there are some basic rules for facing the media you should know:

(1) Remember—there is no such thing as "off the record." You may doubt this for a long time because your favourite reporter never goes to camera with what you told her in confidence. But someday, when the story is

big enough, you will be burned. Reporters are paid, promoted and given awards for telling stories, not keeping secrets.

(2) Always go into an interview with one or two messages you wish to leave with the audience. The reporter is a conduit, not an audience.

(3) Repeat those messages as often as possible. Don't be shy about giving your message even if you have to use a shoehorn. "That's a good question, Sam. I was hoping you'd ask about our record year first, but let me answer your question…" It takes a little practice, but there's not much sense doing interviews without a purpose.

(4) Get in the habit of allowing a brief pause before you answer any question. When you need that split second to react to a surprise question, it will not be obvious if the little pause is part of your normal rhythm.

(5) Avoid television interviews where you are in one location facing a single camera and the interviewer is remote in another studio. It is very difficult for you at the satellite end to seem natural in this setup—which is precisely why some news broadcasters like it. They control the event totally.

(5) If you suspect that the interview will put you in a defensive situation, get colleagues to ask you tough questions in advance. It is amazing how much easier it is to deal with a mean-spirited query when you've already heard it asked out loud and given an answer. Without

such advance toughening most people feel brutalized by rough questions and lose their self-possession. In political circles such rehearsals are known as "dirty Q's and N's."

PROBLEM EMPLOYEES

Our employees are human beings, which is what brings the challenge to managing. Human beings will bring to work with them a host of different attitudes, styles, prejudices, ambitions, fears and hopes. Some of these will create problems that affect work performance—of the employee and co-workers.

And you.

Many managers feel they must also be mothers and fathers, counsellors and rehab leaders. Too much of this approach, however well intentioned, eventually turns the office or plant floor into a sick bay. The effective manager knows when an employee's actions damage performance and/or begin to create discomfort for others. It might be the drunk who expects others to cover for him, or the mean-tempered office supervisor who has support staff cowering rather than creating.

Whatever the problem, there are rules that will help you meet your responsibilities as a manager:

(1) Do not put off resolving an employee problem; it will not disappear on its own. Sure, it is easier to be the sympathetic confidant for the employee with a problem, but this usually isn't the best management choice. Problems on the job are like cancers; the longer they remain, the more they affect the areas around them. You have a perfect right to ensure the problem employee is not impeding the efforts of others.

(2) If you are acting on reports rather than personal observation, be absolutely certain of the facts before you have any discussion with the problem employee. If you muff the first encounter, it is difficult to recover.

(3) Be clear what behavioural changes you expect. Hazy "try and loosen up" requests don't work. At the next interview, your employee will say he tried, which is all you asked. Instead, say, "Henry, the next time you come in after lunch with liquor on your breath, we'll put an official warning on the file. Without question. Do you understand that?" The more specific the demand you make, the easier it is to monitor performance and follow up.

(4) Resist the temptation to tell your other employees how you dealt with the problem—what rules were laid down, what shoulder was offered to cry on. Helping an

employee deal with a problem should be a very private and personal exchange.

(5) Prepare yourself with advice from doctors or Human Resources specialists if you believe the employee's problem is deep-seated. This is fair to the employee as well as to you. For example, if the worker's difficulty stems from serious depression, it may be beyond the worker to comply with any requests you make. So get outside medical professional assistance.

(6) Conduct your discussions in the employee's office or a common meeting room. Do not use your own office. That way the employee won't feel he or she has been "called in." As well, if the meeting is upsetting, the employee has a place to recover.

None of the rules should stampede the manager into cold-blooded robot-like reactions to employees who cause problems. There should always be room for human understanding and sympathy—but not at the cost of making other employees inefficient or uncomfortable. You are the conductor of an orchestra. When one instrument is out of tune, you have to decide when that affects the overall performance.

POLITICAL INVOLVEMENT

Most organizations are asked to contribute time and money to political parties and candidates at all levels, from municipal to federal. Your organization should have a position on its involvement.

Regardless of what that position is, you, as a talented manager, should consider your own participation in politics. You might argue that you are too busy, but it is hard to place personal involvement in a democracy at the bottom of your priority list.

If you decide to take part directly in election campaigns, here are some guidelines:

(1) Treat political campaigns as test labs for ideas you have on managing people. Take a group of strangers, give them a common cause and see how much work you can

get out of them without financial compensation. And in a few weeks the assignment is completed.

(2) If you want to be efficient and get the largest personal return from campaigns, be the fundraiser. You can do most of the work on the phone on your own timetable. You get to work with the true insiders—the money people. Once you get over the challenge of asking for money and learn that it's a standard part of business and politics, fundraising is painless. It certainly is easier than phoning friends and asking them to spend two or three weeks knocking on doors and delivering pamphlets in the rain.

(3) Use the campaign for identifying possible recruits for your organization. Here is a pressure-filled, value/mission-driven entity. What better circumstance could there be for assessing people? And at no cost for the assessment.

Watch who handles their campaign assignments effectively. Who meets deadlines? Who sells their views to the group? Who gets up off the floor first when there is a campaign setback, as there will be?

(4) In a campaign setting you can practise your own presentation and persuasion skills. Nobody has to listen to you as they might at work. You have to invent yourself as a campaigner. If you try to lead a group of volunteers and they don't like your approach, they stay home. That may be painful, but it's instructive.

(5) Remember, not everybody in your organization

will support the same party. You may have colleagues who work for political candidates opposing yours. If you can't live comfortably with this (with a touch of humour and perhaps some friendly chiding), don't get involved in politics.

HOT FADS
AND HOW TO
IGNORE THEM

You will be challenged constantly to try new methods of managing, leading, presenting, listening, creating. If you don't like today's ideas, hold tight. Tomorrow will bring a whole new batch of flipchart miracles.

Better yet, wait ten years, and you'll get today's brilliant concepts back again. There aren't many truly new ideas for dealing with people. As I said at the start of this book, people don't change much.

Here are a few ways to deal with new (and old) ideas:

(1) When a consultant or behavioural scientist pitches you a new surefire way to improve your work, ask for a clear, concise report on how the new method has affected the pitcher's organization. Unless the answer is right on the tip of her/his tongue, conclude the meeting. If it ain't

good enough for them, it ain't good enough for you. At least 90% of the people who try to sell you training or change ideas will not be able to demonstrate they use it themselves. What shocking gall.

(2) Do not be afraid to ask the big guys the same question. When the first edition of this book appeared, one of the world's largest consulting firms was falling apart because one division invaded another division's turf. They couldn't find a resolution; they couldn't keep it out of the press. Yet they still felt confident telling you how to manage your organization and image. Help them learn a little humility.

Take a second look at how many company cases were actually cited as the basis for the big bestseller *Reengineering the Corporation,* by Hammer and Champy. Check out how many of those were actually known to the authors firsthand. The statistical base of organizations noted isn't big enough to project across the street, let alone across the world of business. In fact, if you read the early part of Champy's later book, he says, in effect, "Hey, you didn't believe all that we said, did you? If you did, here's another book to help you repair the damage." The incredible thing is, he made money on both books!

(3) Here's a terrific idea if you want to do some team-building and basic business training for your people. Go out and find two or three small businesses in a start-up phase. Invite them to make presentations on their busi-

nesses to your management group. Pay them to prepare and present these outlines. Now divide your group into teams and have them offer advice to the small businesses on every aspect of their operations. This will get your teams back to basics.

You may want a panel of judges to comment on your teams' work. For example, if your enterprise is suffering from a lack of customer focus, the teams might all be weak in this area in their recommendations to the small businesses.

(4) Don't approve any "think-in" or retreat that lasts longer than two days. If your staff can go away and be out of touch for more than two days, they don't need training, you need staff reductions. Assume when staff are at a training program, they will concentrate on that. No phone calls, no nervous assistants creeping into the room to hunker down beside their boss while memos are scanned.

(5) Demand from every participant at every improvement exercise a one-page note stating how the program will help them in business, day by day, starting this very day. Remind future advocates, internal or external, as they present new program ideas, that they will be judged by what those results notes tell you.

The results notes are about lessons learned. They are not the same as the commonly used evaluation forms asking about room temperature, slide quality and menus.

(6) Training or improvement seminars, retreats and so on become more effective and useful to the company in direct proportion to the number of different divisions and levels of management included. We already know everything the guy in the next office thinks.

Watch for senior executives who think they are too important to mix with the troops in such events. They are insecure or snobs. This needs attention. The common method for avoiding attendance, as practised by the timid top, is to sign up and then plead press of business at the last minute.

TRADE ASSOCIATIONS

Your trade association is as good as you make it. That means if you work actively for your trade association, it will return benefits to your industry. If you don't plan to be involved and help direct the association, don't join.

If the association isn't worth your time, it isn't worth your money.

When an industry or sector has several associations, you have no obligation to support them all. In fact, supporting the weaker or fringe associations only serves to dilute the industry's voice to government or the public. In Canada, for example, the membership in one trade association accounts for 95% of total industry revenues; there are thirteen other trade associations in the same industry. Each of the fourteen groups claims to speak for the industry.

Imagine trying to get a unified response to a sudden shift in government policy. Think how easy it is for government to find at least one association in the industry that favours the government view.

If your organization does belong to more than one association—for example, your industry association plus the Chamber of Commerce—assign one person to each association to take a leadership role. Then ensure your representative is recognized for this outside work. It is a serious delegation of responsibility, and time and resources should be allotted to this industry effort. You may want to try an up-and-coming executive with some association work on your behalf. It is an excellent testing ground that allows you to see people demonstrate their capacity to lead by persuasion.

Be Loyal

Your organization may be large enough to get the ear of the government or the public directly without the help of a trade association. If this is the case, you have a responsibility not to work at cross purposes with your association. In recent years this has been seen most clearly when trade associations called for government to reduce grants to the private sector. At the very same time member companies of these associations were lining up at the grant window. What was government or the citizen in the street to think of that?

This facile approach to association responsibility is like holding up a bank on the way home from church.

Pay close attention to the materials your trade association produces. Much of this is high quality, particularly the articles intended for use with your employees. If your organization is not using these materials, find out why. If the answer is that the material isn't good enough, then have the association improve it.

Often you will discover that association bulletins and communications tools are ignored simply because they didn't originate in your organization. This means you are paying twice for many of your employee messages—once for your people to do the work and once for your trade association to do the work.

Dating Service

Trade associations offer an unmatched opportunity for networking. In a world where strategic alliances are becoming a common method of doing business, the trade association is a perfect dating service.

Finally, the better associations have an ear to the ground for changing public opinion. They are fed information by members. Special interest groups talk to them. This means that your association can provide the continuing environmental scan today's business organizations need.

Your trade association has much in common with your own business and personal associates. You want to choose it carefully and then treat it with respect and affection.

WHEN A FRIEND IS OUT OF WORK

Some of your friends will be fired, laid off or organized out of a decent job now and then.

They will want your help. They may not ask for it in plain words, particularly if things are booming for you. Friends will want to avoid any appearance of using you.

Remember here, we are talking about most normal professional friends. There are others who, far from being bashful about asking for help, will almost demand it as their due. These are the ones who were fired probably because they don't want to work if they can get somebody else to do it for them. Don't spend a lot of time worrying about these people.

For the good ones, have communications available. Today, when people are wired to the world from home, this is not as big a problem as it used to be. However, don't take it for granted. Ask if they have the resources to produce resumes, follow-up letters and all the panoply of materials essential to a successful job search.

Take the out-of-worker to lunch regularly at industry hangouts. Don't let your friend fall out of business society. Let them pay if they offer. They are having trouble deep down grappling with losing their job and don't need poverty rubbed in their face.

Once when I came back from Europe after resigning from a job, money was a little tight. A friend took my wife and me to dinner and paid for the entire evening with new $100 bills. One for each round of drinks, some for dinner, another for liqueurs. I never forgave him.

Make sure your out-of-worker has a bathroom to use. Nothing is harder for an executive than to have to put a quarter in the toilet booth at the bus station and then try to be psychologically up for an interview. So if you are conveniently located, lend a fresh-up place to your friend.

Never expect people to be grateful for your help. Many times women and men out of work will reveal to you more than they really wish about their fears and anxieties. They don't want to face these thoughts again when things are going well. So they may tune you out—a reminder of bad days.

THIRTEEN TIPS FOR MARKETING LUCK

(1) Always keep learning. You and the organization must stay ahead, not just abreast of the times. Don't skimp on budgets for training. Do have formal, written, personal growth plans from every member of the marketing team.

(2) Research is your best friend. Use it properly and it will make you a professional.

(3) Learn to present your case to one or a hundred. The best marketing plan in the world does nobody any good unless it gets approved and into action.

(4) Improve your writing skills. Try going back six months in your files and read notes or memos you wrote. Assess how the writing stands up now that you have some distance from the original passion for the subject.

(5) Nurture and cherish creative talent. If you find a great copy writer, that is, one who never does poor stuff and sometimes does great stuff, treat him or her like gold. Once I created a fund that allowed copy writers to test ideas my own organization had turned down. That way the writers had a chance to say, "I told you so." Remember, account executives are paid to love you. Writers aren't.

(6) Bubble good ideas from juniors right to the top. Even if you have made considerable improvements to an idea that started with one of your staff, make sure everybody knows who originated it. The creator will be thrilled.

(7) Never turn tail on your team. Once it has agreed on a plan or course of action, fly high or crash together. In the face of opposition from higher management, the team leader must be a team member, too.

(8) Study every breath your competitors take.

(9) Be wildly enthusiastic about contributions of your team-mates. It takes zero courage to say "no" to ideas. It takes nerve to be totally on side. Practise saying, "That's a terrific idea. Let's do it!"

(10) If you have an advertising agency, be the best client it ever had. The other clients are competing for the agency's best thinking and you need it.

(11) Examine, analyse and discuss advertising from everywhere in the world. Advertising is one of our

valuable tools and we must sharpen its edges constantly—one way is to watch what others are doing. *Note to smaller organizations: the tinier the budget, the less room for error. Continual improvement of your advertising makes every dollar go farther by making it more effective.*

(12) You can't eat percentages. Many marketers attempt to use formula marketing programs based on percentages—for example, media spending should be 30% of sales for over-the-counter drugs. This leads to frustration because percentages don't work for smaller organizations. Don't get trapped by formulas. Figure out what you must spend to compete and win. Then, if you must, calculate the percentage.

(13) Keep your sense of humour and you'll keep your sanity.

PUBLICLY
RELATING

Members of the public are going to have an impression of your company. They will form this impression from their dealings with you, what they may see and hear in the press, their uncles' tales, the shareholders' meeting, the thirty-five years they have worked for the company. However they form their view of your company, people will have one.

Whether that overall view is positive or negative is important. If consumers don't like your company, they won't buy your products (look at the massive consumer reaction to environmentally unfriendly products). If governments don't trust you, then your applications for product approvals, favourable tax rulings, a government minister to open a new plant, are all on shaky ground. If talented prospects don't want to come and work for you, ultimately your company dies. So, to put it mildly, image is important.

Fortunately, if you are doing a good job treating consumers as friendly masters, much of the image making takes care of itself. Ongoing consumer research should also be alerting you to changing attitudes out there so you can be ahead of the curve. Generally speaking, doing the right thing brings its own rewards.

Still, you need to know the rules for public relations. If you don't need them for your own company, use them when you are chairperson of your industry association.

(1) Never say anything in any meeting you wouldn't like to see on television that night.

(2) When major problems strike, your top executive must be the public spokesperson. That shows your entire company cares and nobody is hiding from responsibility. This is also why your top people have to be ready, through earlier training, to get on air, stand at the podium or face the scrum at very short notice.

(3) Don't try to use the media for free publicity by sending a constant stream of news releases that are mostly interesting to you. When you finally do have something to say, there won't be anybody in the media ready to listen.

(4) Do not assume being an important advertiser will buy any favours with the media.

(5) If you have an industry association, be active in it so you have a voice in what is said to government and the public. It's part of your image.

(6) Insist that plans for major activities by the company, such as plant closings, include communications plans. And remember, communications plans should include employees as a key audience.

(7) If you have funds available to support community programs or charities, ask your employees which efforts they wish to support. They earn the money and should have a say in where it goes.

(8) You are better off with one top public relations person in-house rather than two or three spear carriers. Outside help can be bought on a project basis. Only a really good PR person will be able to fill a chair at management meetings—an essential to effective PR for the company.

(10) Don't confuse public relations with product publicity. They are different activities.

(11) Your company should have an annual public relations plan just as it has plans for other activities. PR is not just a reactive mechanism. Think about PR as the cheapest way to ensure top prospects are waiting to join your company—that's one way to put a value on the effort. (The Communications Power Grid, page 16, is incredibly effective as a PR planning tool.)

GOVERNMENT RELATIONS

You have a responsibility to work to improve government. As citizens, we all have that responsibility. It is our government, it is important, and we must always be active in helping government do better.

You can work through a trade association or directly, or both. Either way there are some key imperatives for dealing with government on any issue any time.

First, remember that dealing with government is a marketing proposition, like so many other aspects of business. That means we need to know the audience. The audience is two-part: the political and the bureaucratic.

These two groups do not always share the same aims, or if they do, the emphasis and the fine print may be different. Still, both groups react to marketing that meets their needs, and we must study each carefully before beginning any campaign to get government to do our will on large or small endeavours.

The Political Side

I long ago created the *Commandments for Dealing with Cabinet Ministers*:

(1) Remember that the minister wants to be reelected.

(2) Remember that the minister wants the government to be reelected.

(3) Remember the order of (1) and (2).

That is the atmosphere in which one markets to ministers and the rest of the political side of government. Always lead with why your proposal is good politics for them, not why it is good for you or your group or sector.

Example: "Here is a way to create twenty-seven jobs in your riding. You can be the creator of a new national call centre in St. John which will train and employ these people. All we need is an agreement between you and the province to allow…"

The fact that your company will make a lot of money by moving its call centre to a low-rent, low-pay area is not the lead line. Get to it, but only after you have the politician's attention.

This may seem like a too-simple illustration. It isn't. The largest deals and arrangements made with government start with such a script. Companies hire government-relations firms to keep abreast of current "hot boxes"—jobs, deficit reduction, downsizing—in government. That lets you know what to lead with and helps the political level see how your need fits their agenda. Then you can share the need and the gratification.

The Bureaucracy

Marketing to the bureaucracy is changing as governments downsize. There are fewer people to think about your idea or project or proposal. There are also fewer people to get your proposal through the process to a successful conclusion.

Good marketing to government bureaucracies today means getting in there and helping the officials who are hard-pressed to cope. Here are some of the major ways to do that:

(1) You know the government needs to hear from several constituencies (sometimes hundreds) on most agenda items. Help by bringing more than one constituency into the fold before you approach government. The insurance companies and the hospitals and the dentists and a host of others found a basic common cause when the government threatened to tax employee health plans. They settled their small differences before going to gov-

ernment. There was no room left for divide-and-conquer or delay to talk to other groups, because almost the entire health-care industry was at the table. And they won.

(2) Governments at all levels are now short of time and people to do long-term thinking—that is, seeing how your proposal dovetails with other government initiatives and, I might add, to their laurels. We must help the bureaucracy with the longer view. I call it *Far Horizon Marketing.* Show how your idea will gather adherents as it flows through the system. Guarantee public support from your sector. Write the draft of the terrific speech the minister will give at the announcement of your plant, phone centre, ballet company, helicopter purchase. Do the positive thinking for the bureaucrats who are not in a positive mood these days as they cope with downsizing.

(3) Be prepared and willing to be helpful to government when they need a hand. When a commission or task force or high-tech conference needs help, be there. When government does something right, shout out your approval in speeches, employee bulletins and through trade associations. Take an official to lunch and don't ask for anything.

(4) In general, remember that our government employees are going through times of crisis and seem to have no friends. Be one. It is the right thing to do as a citizen. It is the smart thing to do as a businessperson.

THE GREAT
MARKETING PLAN HOAX

The marketing plan. The greatest accomplishment of two or three generations of MBA graduates has been to convince the world that the Marketing Plan is a cross between a voodoo rite and an Einstein equation.

Don't believe it.

A marketing plan is, essentially, an application for a loan. It's a request to use resources controlled by somebody else to fuel an activity of yours. Whether it's a plan to sell lemonade on a street corner or jet liners in Korea, there are four questions to be answered and they are always the same:

(1) How much money do we need?

(2) What do we need the money for?

(3) What assurances can we give that the money will be repaid?

(4) When will the money be repaid?

The amount of detail in each answer will vary with the institution involved. So will the amount of verbiage. Still, the basics will remain: Answer the questions and get the loan (or the use of the resources); don't answer the questions and fail.

You could write a marketing plan right now if you answered those questions.

You could also write a *Business Plan*. Don't believe that a business plan is a complicated document, either. A Business Plan is a Marketing Plan in which the whole business is the product. That's it. So answer the questions. You have a plan.

(1) How much money do we need?

The answer to this is often "How long is a piece of string?" This is not a good answer.

The correct answer for the question, within a marketing plan, is usually twofold. "We need this much money if you want repayment fast. We need less if you can wait a while."

Either way the amount needed is the sum of the costs of each and every activity surrounding the marketing of a product or an idea. Advertising. Manufacturing. Promotion. Commissions. Packaging. Product. Legal fees. And more.

Put the costs down, line by line. Always add, and show, a plus or minus percentage of 10% to the estimates.

Do this for each item, not just once, so it isn't so easy for the banker to take it away.

Never count on luck. If you are selling suntan lotion, don't base your plan on a sunny summer this year. Base your cost on the amount of suntan lotion sold in an average year for the past decade. Then put an asterisk on your budget and tell the banker how a bad summer could affect total volume and thus your costs.

No luck and no surprises. A potential problem shared with the banker at the outset is a problem you both own. The one you don't mention becomes your exclusive property, and your credibility is in question to boot.

There are lots of reasons to cross your fingers in business. Don't create more on purpose.

(2) What do we need the money for?

Well, here's where you tell the great idea. The new hair grower. The killer app. The electric potato peeler. A new board game.

Why is the idea good? Is it similar to something that's already successful? Is there some indication people want this idea/product? How big is the market category? Is there research showing a hole or niche in the market?

What you want to do here is answer this subquestion: "Why this product/idea at this time in this place?" It is always best to answer obvious questions in advance. Simple tests will often do and they are certainly better than none. "Some of the people who may want this product are seniors. Have you thought of that?" "As a matter of fact, the major problem seniors have with our competitor's product is the lid is hard to get off—our lid pops off. Even my eighty-year-old mother finds it easy." Then be ready for the other question: Is it childproof?

All the reasons that this product/idea solves a problem or fills a need should be detailed.

Sometimes enthusiasm for the product yields unexpected results. Once, the marketing plan for a new paint roller I was involved with was being pitched to Bay Street insiders with money to invest. The meeting was delayed when one of the mighty moguls slipped away to phone his wife. He wanted to tell her to postpone the paint job at home until he could get one of our rollers.

(3) What assurances can we give that the money will be repaid?

This is where "the rubber meets the road" as they used to say on Madison Avenue. In this part of a marketing plan goes the outline of what smart things we have done and are going to do to guarantee the success of our product.

The thing to remember here is that the plans and the amount of detail are expressed differently in different situations. To be blunt, never tell more than the lender can comprehend.

For instance, if you are planning a new product launch within an empire such as General Foods or Procter & Gamble, you will want to include not only an advertising strategy but also a copy strategy (the way your advertising will be unique and competitive). The lenders in those companies will understand and their faith will increase if they embrace your strategy.

But if you give the average bank manager the details of a copy strategy within an advertising strategy within a marketing strategy, you have simply created a communications barrier. The banker doesn't understand, isn't happy, doesn't like you anymore.

Market research should be in this section of the plan. The research does not need to be awfully expensive or sophisticated. It does need to be described for what it is. A telephone survey of a hundred consumers should not be billed as extensive probing of the marketplace. Come on. The lender is your partner. Tell it like it is. If the market assessment has you excited, why won't it excite somebody else? And if it doesn't, isn't that a reason for you to pause before launching yourself through the air towards the flaming hoop?

Tell the lender about promotion plans and distribution plans. If you need supermarket distribution, for example, have you reason to believe any of the big chains will accept your product? Have you money built into the budget to buy your way in?

Talk about advertising, public relations, relations with key business columnists.

This part of the plan is "credentials in action." You're asked, "You think you know how to sell this? Okay, tell me how."

(4) When will the money be repaid?

Boy. This is the tough one. Remember, we already said the amount needed depended on the speed of return. There is nothing wrong with presenting more than one repayment plan.

One plan has to be the conservative, low-risk approach. So we put down the costs. We estimate revenues. We then calculate the point at which revenues will exceed costs sufficiently to pay back our loan. We also agree to checkpoints along the way, where we compare plans to results and take appropriate action. Never let this discipline be initiated by the lender. Put it in the plan.

The other repayment plan is the aggressive, prime-the-pump attack plan. For many products today this is, in fact, the only way to market. The capacity to copy products means if you don't get into the market fast and take your share, you won't get that share. The speed of innovation also means your product may be outmoded if you don't penetrate the market quickly.

The two plans may very well end up with the same repayment date. Plan A repays the loan in five years; so does plan B. The difference is that the hyper plan puts lots of money at risk right away. It is not a pay-as-we-grow program.

A classic illustration of this is the drug company that goes to market with two new products. One is a breakthrough prescription cholesterol fighter; the other is an over-the-counter painkiller in the very competitive analgesic market.

The prescription drug, whose heavy production costs have been absorbed in company overhead, goes to market with some modest print advertising in medical journals and a new sample kit for the medical sales force. For the painkiller the drug company must spend millions of dollars in advertising just to be heard above the competition.

On the Marketing Plan projections these products will have very different dates for showing a profit.

Now we sit with the lender, look at the market research together and decide on an approach. If we decide on the hit-hard blitzkrieg and the lender wants to nickel-and-dime it, get out. Only if we have a solid mutual understanding of the mechanics of the marketplace and what it takes to play, can we and our lender face the future together. Cold feet have to be warmed in advance.

Put this concept on the table: advertising and promotion dollars are part of the product. Too often lenders get antsy after six months, or perhaps when they see some competitor interviewed on television, and try to cut promotional budgets. Often the dollars are not yet spent or we can buy out of contracts, so the money is tantalizingly available. From the outset lenders must understand that promotion is what drives the repayment of the loan. To put our balloon in the air and then cut off the hot air guarantees a crash.

THE
SELECTION INTERVIEW

Our people are our most important resource" or similar phrases are voiced, and meant, every day by business leaders. It is strange indeed then just how little attention we pay to the interviews that usually decide which people will join our organization.

Very few managers are trained to interview potential new members of the management team. It's an incredible gap in our total business system.

Think about it.

We are making decisions of monumental importance to a candidate's life. We are making decisions of great importance to our organization's future. But we get more training on handling the new telephone system than we do in conducting effective interviews.

Here are the rules for interviewing manager aspirants:

(1) Placing a person in the wrong job is a sin against both that person and the organization. So don't be afraid to ask probing questions. This is business, not a social occasion.

(2) Decide in advance what the organization or team demands of its managers. Is it creative independence? Compliance with rules? Heroic hours of work? Those are the sort of attributes you want to look for that will not be revealed in a resume.

(3) Determine if the candidate has had some control of his or her own destiny. If the potential manager has simply been carried along, there is no track record of leadership or planning capacity. Ask, for example, a question like this: "Tell me, Mary, what is the biggest decision you ever made?" Followed by: "How did you go about making that decision?" You need to find out if the candidate takes responsibility for past events.

(4) If you ask, "What rules did you break in your last job?" and then "Why did you do that and would you do it again?" this may result in some tension. Good. This candidate is somebody you are going to share your professional life with, and tension will be a regular occurrence. So try it on.

(5) Do your homework in advance. It is insulting to a candidate if you're busy studying the resume during the

interview. You should have read it, designed your interview accordingly and be ready to go. This candidate may be a future president of your organization. Let that guide your approach to the interview—it is serious for both sides of the desk.

(6) Speaking of desks, don't interview across one. Get that barrier out of the way. Sit at a meeting table or a coffee table. Create psychological equality as much as possible. This is a conversation between potential colleagues, not an inquisition.

(7) Lunchrooms and restaurants are not suitable sites for interviews unless you are especially concerned with a candidate's table manners. It is simply not fair to expect a candidate to listen, absorb and respond to probing questions in competition with servers, friendly passersby and dropped plates.

(8) Talk to your colleagues about interviewing. Try to get some practice sessions going and develop a consistent corporate approach to interviewing.

Choosing people may be the most important job you do. Treat the process accordingly.

THANK YOU,
THANK YOU,
THANK YOU

You are measured by the amount of .gratitude you show people—especially those who can't do anything important for you. Always try to say thanks to those who deserve it.

A note sent immediately to an assistant who arranged a meeting with her boss is much appreciated. A bunch of flowers is good if it would not embarrass its receiver.

And don't be stingy with thanks to your own team when they come through at a presentation. "Thanks, Larry, that was great," as you walk down the hall to the elevator is all it takes to make Larry feel good. Putting the thanks in such a way makes it a gesture of gratitude rather than simply a professional critique. There's a difference.

Politicians have learned, or are staffed, to say thanks to many folks along the way. They thank the "little people" on the phones every time they walk into a headquarters point. They thank volunteers at every meeting. They send notes to financial contributors. This may be the most important lesson a businessperson can learn from politicians—thank-yous are the secret lubricant keeping many organizations performing well.

You can also say thanks to people by mentioning their efforts to others. For example, "Thanks for making time to see us, Mr. Smith, and I must say, Helen made the arrangements for this meeting about as smoothly as I've ever seen." Helen will hear about it probably, but that's not the point. You really want to thank Helen, and praising her to the president is one way to do it.

There is an exception to the "always say thank you" rule. It is the exception that is broken more often than the rule. Here it is. Do not say "thank you" at the end of a speech.

The audience should have received the best you have to give during the speech. Your thoughts and the coherent organization and delivery of them are the thanks you give for the audience's time. They are supposed to thank *you* for that.

Write a closing sentence people will remember.

Deliver it. Then leave the podium.

EMAIL
IS NOW
A FACT OF LIFE

The good news with the Internet and with email as a written-word transmitter is that we return to the days when writing a cognizant note or letter was important. Hurray.

The bad news is that everybody loads up our electronic in-basket. It seems every thought crossing some people's minds gets transmitted. This is often because email works at any time, and so the crazies in the company can send us stuff at midnight.

Email tends to destroy discrimination in what is sent.

In your own organization make people declare a priority and put it in the subject line.

"Urgent" should mean urgent. "Important" should mean heavy-duty news.

This will also give you a new way to judge an individual's understanding of the business. Just watch what people declare as urgent or important. Counsel them on the difference between important to them and important to you and the organization.

And never read anything in the system until you have done the "urgents" and "importants." Otherwise you have no right to ask for the self-declaration by others.

A HANDFUL OF BRIEFS ON A VARIETY OF THINGS

Conferences

When any employee goes to a paid training program or industry conference, the first task on returning is to create a note for colleagues on ideas or information from the meeting. This note should include a recommendation on future participation in the event or program.

Expense accounts for the meetings should not be approved until the reporting note is circulated.

Networking

Much is made of networking for personal career enhancement. It works for the organization, too. Every industry luncheon, every meeting of a professional society, every trade association gathering, trade show or United

Way committee is a place to look for recruits, strategic partners, information sources and suppliers. These are events and occasions that are work, not relaxation, so keep your organizational hat firmly in place.

Conformity

However much you may champion individual creativity, people in an organization should conform to some formal guidelines. Chief among these should be a common format for certain memos and documents going through the system. You should not have to claw your way through a host of individual writing styles and formats to discover an idea. Assessing ideas is work enough without having to search for those ideas lurking in the camouflage of wordy memos. Declare a format for certain documents and set out the headings. Workers will live with this if it means getting ideas rewarded faster.

Completed Staff Work

An old concept that should be brought back to the workplace is "completed staffwork." This means, when you send a recommendation forward, it is complete with draft letters or notes to advance the idea to the next step. If the recommendation is that the president should write to the prime minister, then the president's letter, ready for signature on the proper letterhead, should accompany the recommendation. If the president agrees, he just signs. If the recommendation is that the team leader argue a case at the management committee meeting, the notes for the presentation should be attached.

This marvellously effective approach to managing does several things. First, it makes people think recommendations all the way through. Second, it forces time-consuming work down to lower-compensation positions. Third, it helps people at every level think their way into the chair of more senior people and so prepare themselves to occupy that chair.

I still remember the day that as a junior at Procter & Gamble I was told that an idea of mine had reached the president and he'd signed the memo I had written without a single change.

Management Books

New approaches to management come along with every book-publishing season. Most offer a single new idea about management style or method. Listen better. Empower. Satisfy customers. Create habits. In most cases you can inhale 99% of what these books offer by reading the first three chapters only. The first chapter will give you at least 75% of the thoughts. So decide how much time you have to spend on diminishing returns after the early pages.

This is true of the writings of even the great management thinkers. Read a Peter Drucker book. Then read his article for *Fortune* or *Harvard Business Review.* What's in the book that the short article doesn't capture? Not much.

Consultants

Over the years many consultants have been hired by middle management, particularly in government, to validate or endorse the client's own views. It seemed an outsider's opinion was needed to convince top management. Of course there was lots of money to pay for all this. The result is a breed of consultant who does not know how to define a problem, let alone fix it.

So always talk to potential consultants about problems they have eliminated or other results achieved. And always check references.

When you hire a consultant, in most cases you are giving privileged access to your organization. That is serious business.

Set an early review date, keep it and be deadly earnest about that review. Right from the outset consultants should know there is an "eject" button after two or four weeks. Sit down and look at progress, talk about the consultant's style and work habits (are they acting like they own the joint?). If the working partnership is satisfactory, then get on with the assignment.

Suppliers

In many industries suppliers have habitually picked up the tab for lunches, dinners and ball games. This isn't bribery, it's normal commerce. However, it becomes demeaning to the supplier if we assume the right to have the bill paid. If we never reach for the cheque, the supplier becomes a little less equal. And inequality is not what we are looking for in a supplier partner. So keep the psychological balance even. Pay some bills, flip for some, go dutch. It pays.

Bathrooms

Don't talk in them.

Business Meals

There are seminars and books dealing with how to handle eating with business colleagues. In fact, you are never wrong if you simply use normal good manners: be on time; don't talk with your mouth full; don't make a production of paying the bill; turn off your phone.

More important to success is choosing a restaurant with enough space between tables to allow conversation in a normal tone. The purpose of eating together is partly to relax together. Huddling behind menus and whispering in each other's ears may be appropriate for romance but not usually for business—especially at lunch. Get a private room. Order the meal in advance. Have the bar set up. This will allow you to do work with minimum interference by restaurant staff. Or to enjoy doing no work in private.

In foreign countries or when hosting visitors from overseas, we may need specific information about customs and eating habits. Embassies will tell you everything you need to know to avoid offending a guest.

Elevators

Don't talk in them.

Talking with Customers

We are in the era of life-long relationships with customers. We have the capacity to store customer information and reach out easily to single customers or groups of customers.

So every time you communicate with a customer or potential customer, you must get more information so you can sharpen the point of your future communications.

No print advertisement should run without some kind of response panel-coupon, phone number, email invitation.

No television commercial should air without a toll-free telephone number and a reason to call it.

Of course, advertising on social media platforms invites responses by its very nature.

The purpose of advertising is to persuade consumers to choose what you offer ahead of other services or products. When technology allowed you only to talk *at* the customer, you were frustrated. Now you can let the customer talk back. Hurray! So do it.

Find a Comfortable Culture

Some young people get swept from university, particularly business schools, directly into high-pressure, competitive, seventy-five-hour-week environments. At the time it is challenging, like making the varsity team or getting the fellowship. But for many the challenge will change over time into a nightmare. New families demand more time. Organizations flatten and have fewer promotions to offer. Politically motivated staff quotas frustrate top performers. For many reasons the career that looked so tempting at age twenty-one sometimes becomes drudgery by age thirty.

Get out.

If you are a good manager, you will be a good manager in many fields. Of course an IBM manager can run Friends of the Earth. Of course an information manager can counsel an emerging nation. Of course an accountant can become a member of Parliament.

The most important person you have to manage is

yourself. The most crucial career you have to direct is your own. Don't spend your life doing something you don't enjoy.

Take your talent where your heart is.

SOME
PARTING WORDS

You've read some or all of this book. I hope you got your money's worth.

The ideas and rules I covered attach themselves happily to most organizations. People in one organization are much like people in another.

As I said at the beginning, "marketing" is at the heart of all the rules. Think first about the needs of the customer, employee, client, supplier, boss, and your ability to deal with them will improve. This doesn't mean satisfying all needs for all people. It does mean understanding the other person's point of view. In the current vernacular it's "knowing where they are coming from." In marketing terms you might think of your needs vis-à-vis somebody else's needs as "gap analysis" and proceed to close the gap.

All of this will be easier if, as I suggest, you take your talent where your heart is.

P.S. If you want to be ahead of the curve in the next decade of management development discussions, go back to the 1960s. The time has come finally for Robert Greenleaf's "Servant/Leader" concepts. And none too soon.

www.ingramcontent.com/pod-product-compliance
Lightning Source LLC
Chambersburg PA
CBHW031903200326
41597CB00012B/522